GW01454481

Word 365 Page Formatting

EASY WORD 365 ESSENTIALS - BOOK 2

M.L. HUMPHREY

Copyright © 2023 M.L. Humphrey

All Rights Reserved.

ISBN: 978-1-63744-101-5

SELECT TITLES BY M.L. HUMPHREY

WORD 365 ESSENTIALS
Word 365 for Beginners
Intermediate Word 365

EASY WORD 365 ESSENTIALS
Text Formatting
Page Formatting
Lists
Tables
Styles and Breaks
Track Changes

See mlhumphrey.com for more Microsoft Office titles

CONTENTS

Introduction

This book is part of the *Easy Word 365 Essentials* series of titles. These are targeted titles that are excerpted from the main *Word 365 Essentials* series and are focused on one specific topic.

If you want a more general introduction to Word, then you should check out the *Word 365 Essentials* titles instead. In this case, *Word 365 for Beginners* which covers paragraph and page formatting in Word as well as other introductory topics.

But if all you want to learn is how to format paragraphs and pages in Word, then this is the book for you.

Paragraph Formatting

In the last chapter the focus was on how to format individual words. Sure, you can apply that kind of formatting to every word in a document, but the formatting itself happens at the word level. Now it's time to move up to the paragraph level.

Most paragraph formatting options are located in the Paragraph section of the Home tab. Some of the options are also available in the mini formatting menu.

There is also a Paragraph dialogue box that includes the most options which can either be opened by clicking on the expansion arrow in the Paragraph section of the Home tab or by right-clicking in the main workspace and choosing Paragraph from the dropdown menu.

We are not going to cover every single option in the Paragraph section of the Home tab in this book. Multilevel lists, shading, and borders are covered in the next book in the series. As is Sort.

So, without further ado:

Paragraph Alignment

In the bottom row of the Paragraph section of the Home tab there are a series of images that show four lines. If you look closely at those lines you'll see that they represent different alignments. The left-hand one has all lines aligned along the left side, the next one has all lines centered, etc.

These are your alignment choices.

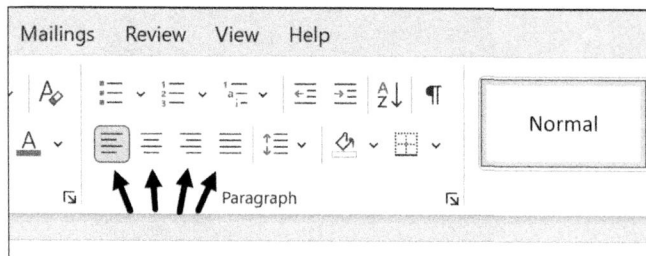

They each also have a control shortcut, which you'll see listed if you hold your mouse over each option. Align Left is Ctrl + L, Center is Ctrl + E, Align Right is Ctrl + R, and Justify is Ctrl + J.

Here are examples of all four:

This is a sample paragraph to show you paragraph alignment. The text in this paragraph is **left-aligned**. I am going to write another sentence here just so we can get to three lines of text. Okay. Done.

This is a sample paragraph to show you paragraph alignment. The text in this paragraph is **centered**. I am going to write another sentence here just so we can get to three lines of text. Okay. Done.

This is a sample paragraph to show you paragraph alignment. The text in this paragraph is **right-aligned**. I am going to write another sentence here just so we can get to three lines of text. Okay. Done.

This is a sample paragraph to show you paragraph alignment. The text in this paragraph is **justified**. I am going to write another sentence here just so we can get to three lines of text. Okay. Done.

Notice that with left- and right-aligned every row lines up along that side but that the opposite side is "ragged" so ends at different points. With centered each row is ragged at both ends and by an equal amount so that the line is centered within that space. With justified the spacing between the words is stretched out so that each row except the last one is lined up on both the left-hand and right-hand side.

Most documents will use either left-aligned or justified paragraphs but centered is often used for things like section headers. Right-aligned I would say is rarely used, at least in languages that read left-to-right, but it can be useful for a side note in a formatted report.

The mini formatting bar is dynamic in Word 365, meaning the choices you see will change on you. By default, I believe your paragraph options will look like this:

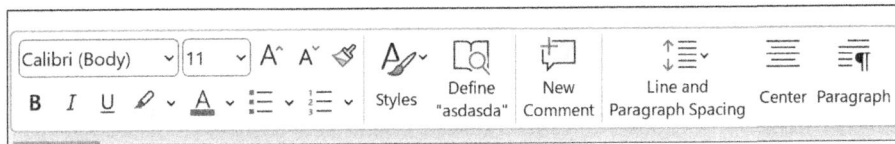

You can see that there is an option for Center, but not the other alignment options.

However, after I was working on this section for a bit, mine looked like this:

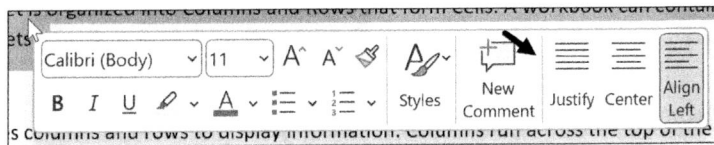

Now I can also see options for Justify and Align Left but the Line and Paragraph Spacing option is gone. At other points I've seen it with options for Center and Justify but not Align Left.

Which to me makes it an option that would not be my first choice. It's there. You can try using it. But the options in the Paragraph section of the Home tab are more consistently available.

Your final paragraph alignment formatting option is the Paragraph dialogue box which you can open by clicking on the expansion arrow in the corner of the Paragraph section of the Home tab. Alignment is available in the top section in a dropdown under General in the Indents and Spacing tab:

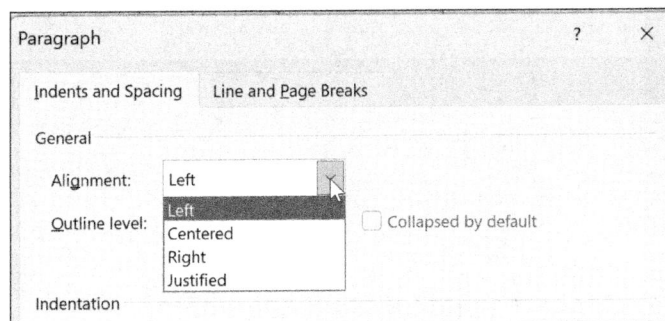

Line Spacing

Throughout school and also with submitting short stories I've always been asked to turn in double-spaced papers. But in the work world double-spaced looks horrible for a final report or memo. So chances are at some point in your life you will need to create a document that uses a different spacing than Word's default, which currently appears to be 1.08.

Here are examples of two paragraphs. The first has the default line spacing of 1.08. The second is double-spaced:

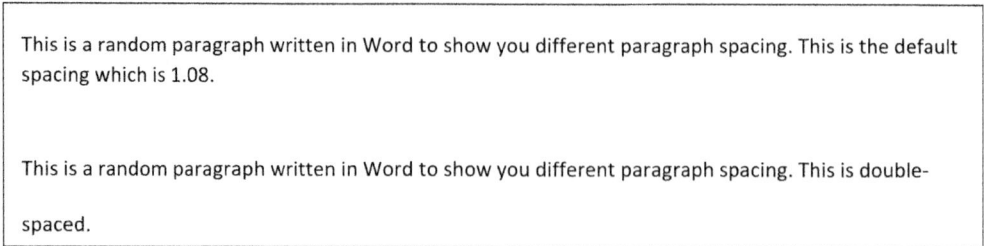

> This is a random paragraph written in Word to show you different paragraph spacing. This is the default spacing which is 1.08.
>
> This is a random paragraph written in Word to show you different paragraph spacing. This is double-spaced.

The way I usually adjust paragraph spacing is to use the Paragraph section of the Home tab. Just to the right of the alignment options in the bottom row is a dropdown menu of choices described as Line and Paragraph Spacing:

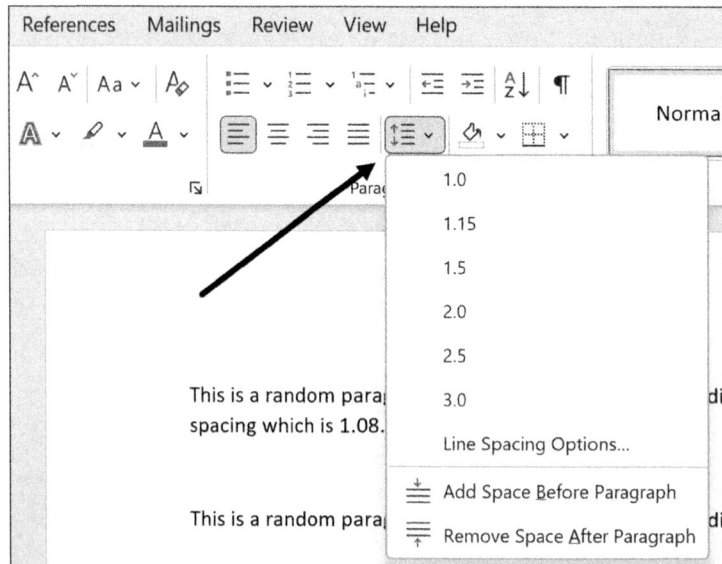

You can hold your mouse over each choice in the list to see what it will look like. Click on a choice to apply it.

If you click on Line Spacing Options in that dropdown it will open the Paragraph dialogue box. Line Spacing is located in the Spacing section on the right-hand side. There is a dropdown menu for Line Spacing there:

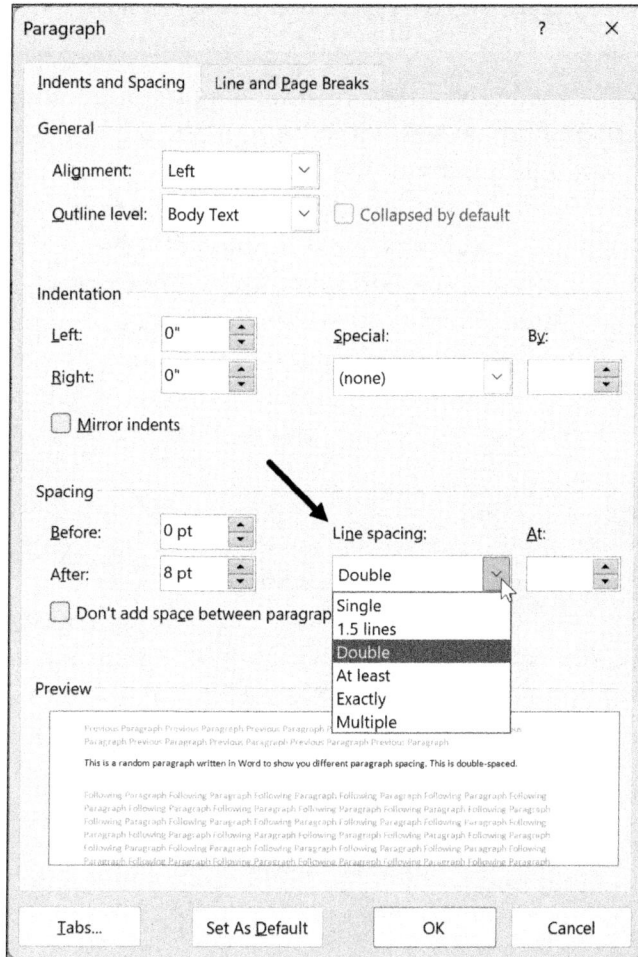

Sometimes I need to use that Exactly option which will then display a font size in the At box that you can adjust.

The mini formatting menu will usually also have the Line and Paragraph Spacing option which uses that same dropdown as in the Paragraph section of the Home tab, but as we saw above, not always.

There are also control shortcuts for paragraph spacing. I personally have never used them because I generally am only using one paragraph format in a document so can just use Ctrl + A to select all and then choose my format from that dropdown menu.

But if you want to use control shortcuts, Ctrl + 1 will give you single-spacing and Ctrl + 2 will give you double-spacing.

Space Between Paragraphs

I mentioned above that sometimes when formatting reports that combined portions written by different team members we'd run across a situation where the sections just didn't quite look the same. Tracking down that difference was a challenge so I'd use the Format Painter to sweep formatting from one paragraph to another. Often what was driving this was a difference in the spacing that was used between paragraphs in those different sections.

Also, this is a very useful setting to use for section headers or chapter headers. The inclination most people have is to use Enter to create space between a header and the text of that section, but the problem is that it doesn't work well when text breaks across a page. You suddenly end up with two blank lines at the top of a page, for example. Using spacing between paragraphs instead is a way to get that distance but not end up with those weird awkward blank lines in your document.

Space between paragraphs is also basically a necessity in the default way that Word formats paragraphs since there are no indents and having that space between your paragraphs is the only way to see that break in your text from paragraph to paragraph.

While the dropdown we just looked at for Line and Paragraph Spacing does have options for adding a space before a paragraph or removing a space after a paragraph, my default is to go straight to the Paragraph dialogue box for this one.

The settings are in the Spacing section on the left-hand side:

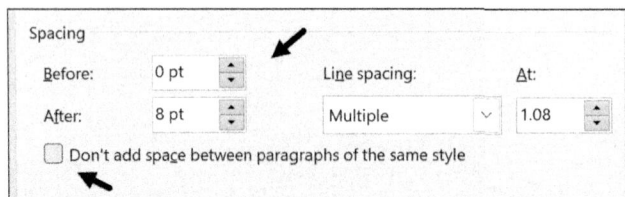

For a chapter header I put a space after. For a section header, though, I will often have values for both before and after. Same for any sort of separator. For me this is a visual setting where you basically play around with the values to see what works well for you.

You can also choose to not include those spaces when dealing with paragraphs of the same style by checking that box there.

Also, if you ever have different spacing at the bottom of one paragraph and at the top of the next, Word will use the larger of the two values, not combine them.

Keep Together

Since we're here and I'm thinking about it, I also want to mention that if you click over to the Line and Page Breaks tab in the Paragraph dialogue box that there are two useful checkboxes there.

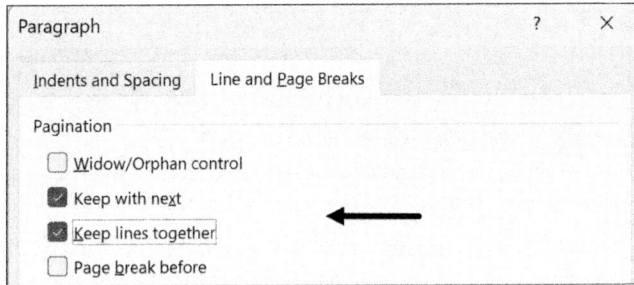

Keep With Next is good for any headers you have in your document because it will make sure that the header stays with the first paragraph of that section. Otherwise you can have a situation where your header is at the bottom of the page and then the text it's actually related to is on the next page, which doesn't look great.

Keep Lines Together is useful for if you have any headers that go across more than one line or if you ever want to make sure that all of the lines in a paragraph are displayed on the same page.

Just know that in order to make these both happen, Word is going to take all of the lines to the next page, which can result in excess white space at the bottom of the previous page. (If you're reading this book in print, you have very likely seen a few examples of that by now. I haven't formatted this book yet, but it happens in every one of these books that there is white space at the bottom of the page either to fit an image or to keep a header and its text together.)

Use these settings, though, to get that effect rather than trying to manually format your report. Because all it takes is someone adding a paragraph earlier in the document to ruin all of that manual formatting and cause you a lot of extra work.

Indents

There are two types of indents to consider. The first is the first-line indent that you see in many books that distinguishes the start of each paragraph. The second is when an entire section or paragraph is indented from the rest of the text.

The indent available in the Paragraph section of the Home tab is the full-section indent. You can click on a paragraph or select a series of paragraphs or bulleted or numbered entries (which we'll discuss in a moment) and then click on the increase indent option and it will move that text in one tab space.

Here I've taken three paragraphs and indented the second one once and the third one twice to show you what that looks like:

(Ignore the text, I was using a book on Microsoft Excel for the text for this one.)

To reverse an indent, use the indent option with the left-pointing arrow in the Paragraph section of the Home tab.

Once I indented those paragraphs the increase and decrease indent options were then also available on the mini formatting menu.

You can also adjust the indent using the Indentation section of the Paragraph dialogue box. See on the left-hand side in the screenshot below where the Left indent is 1". This is also where you need to go to apply a first-line indent to a paragraph.

For the first-line indent, go to the Special option in the Indentation section and click on the dropdown. Select First Line and then type a value into the By field. It's going to default to a .5" indent, but that's generally going to be too much of an indent. Here is a .2" indent where I've also removed the spacing between those two paragraphs:

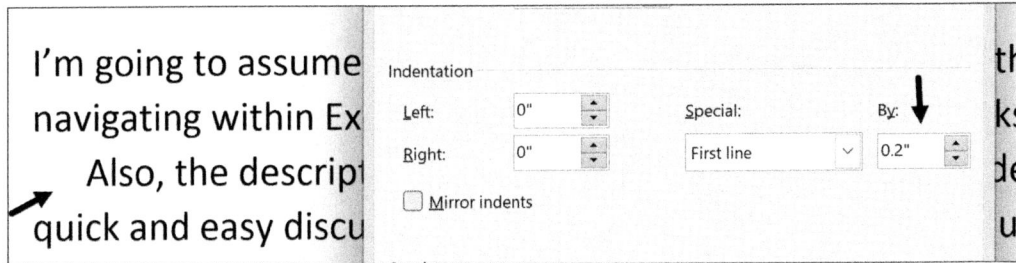

I'm going to assume navigating within Ex Also, the descript quick and easy discu

Indentation
Left: 0"
Right: 0"
Mirror indents
Special: First line
By: 0.2"

In general, you should either have spacing between your paragraphs and no first-line indent or no spacing between paragraphs but use a first-line indent. Don't do both.

Finally, another indenting option is the Tab key (and then Shift + Tab to reverse that), which will indent a single line and will create that first-line indent for you if used on a paragraph. But don't use it. There's more control and consistency in using the Paragraph dialogue box and choosing exactly the type and size of indent you want.

Page and Document Formatting

Okay, that was the paragraph level. Now on to the page and document level. I'm not going to cover everything here, just the basics you need to get started.

Headers and Footers

You can insert text into the header or footer of your document. This is text that is kept separate from the main body of your document. The header is the text at the top of the document, the footer is the text at the bottom.

Often, for example, on a multi-page report you will want to have a header that states the title of the report and maybe the author of the report. Or maybe you want to include a corporate logo on the top of every page.

And usually you'll want a page number in the footer of the document. (Page numbers are covered specifically in the next section.)

To insert a header or footer go to the Header & Footer section of the Insert tab and then click on the dropdown arrow for the one you want. Word will give you a series of choices, some of which are very fancy:

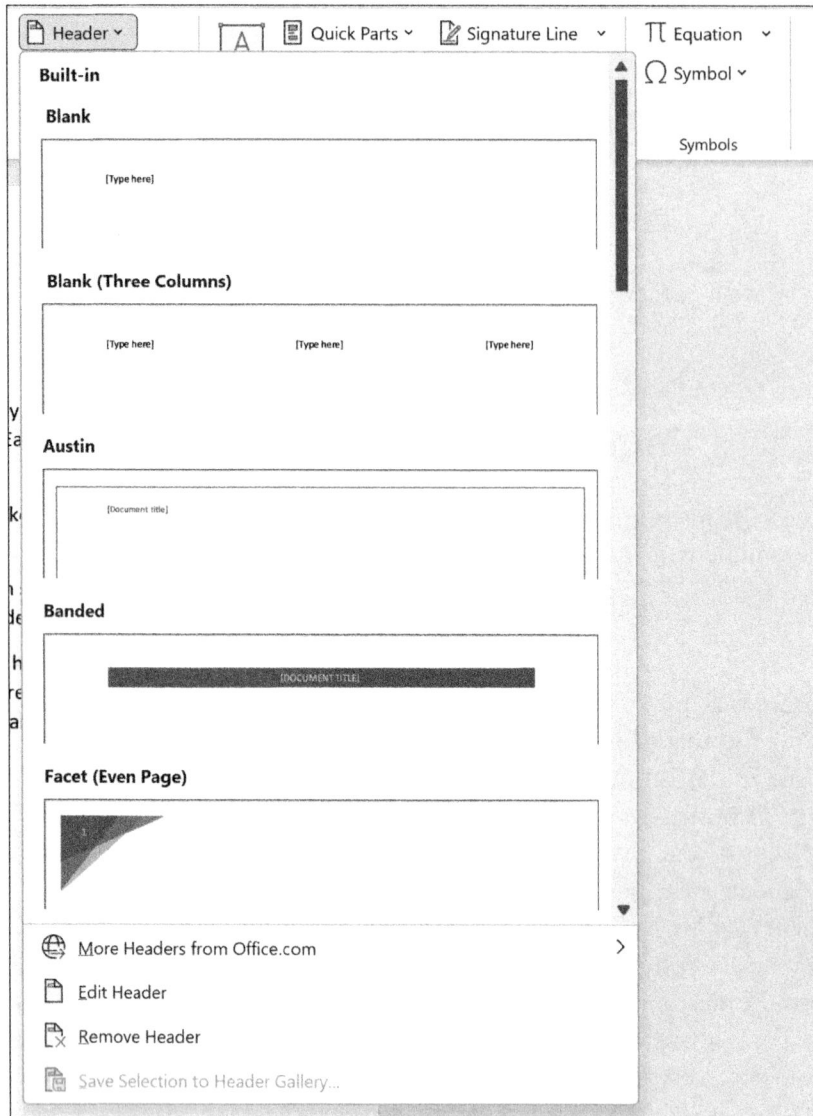

The top two, blank and blank (three columns), are generic choices with no special formatting that allow you to provide your own text in the spots that say [Text here].

The ones below that are fancier. You can also go to the web for even more choices using the Office.com option below the list of built-in choices. The ones that use [Author Name] or [Document Title] are going to pull in properties of the document to populate those particular fields, so be wary of using those.

If you choose one of the blank options it will insert text fields that say [Type here] that you then can click on and delete or replace with text. Here I've entered text for the first of the three-part footer option:

Footer		
Really Important Report	[Type here]	[Type here]

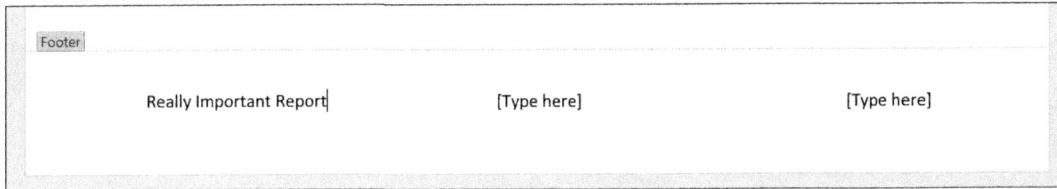

The Insert section of the Header & Footer tab includes options to insert Date & Time information, document information such as Author, File Name, File Path, and Document Title, or pictures. I had one employer where we would regularly insert the corporate logo in the header, for example.

The Options section of the Header & Footer tab also includes checkboxes for if you want a different header or footer for the first page or different header or footer for odd and even pages. I use these often because I usually need to have a different header for the first page of the document since a first-page header usually doesn't include text.

To return to your document from your header or footer, double-click back onto the text of your document or use the Esc key. You can also click on the Close Header and Footer option in the Header & Footer tab.

To return to the header or footer, just double-click on the header or footer text. You can also right-click on that text and choose Edit Header or Edit Footer, whichever option appears. This second option works even when there is no text in that header or footer.

Now let's talk about page numbering.

Page Numbering

First, if you already have a text-based header or footer that you've inserted, you can click into the header or footer and then go to the Page Number dropdown in the Header & Footer section of the Header & Footer tab and choose Current Position to insert a page number there. The top option in the secondary dropdown menu will insert a basic page number, but there are other options shown below that.

If you don't already have a header or footer in your document and you want to insert a page number, go to the Header & Footer section of the Insert tab and click on the Page Number dropdown arrow to see a list of options that include Top of Page, Bottom of Page, Page Margins, and Current Position.

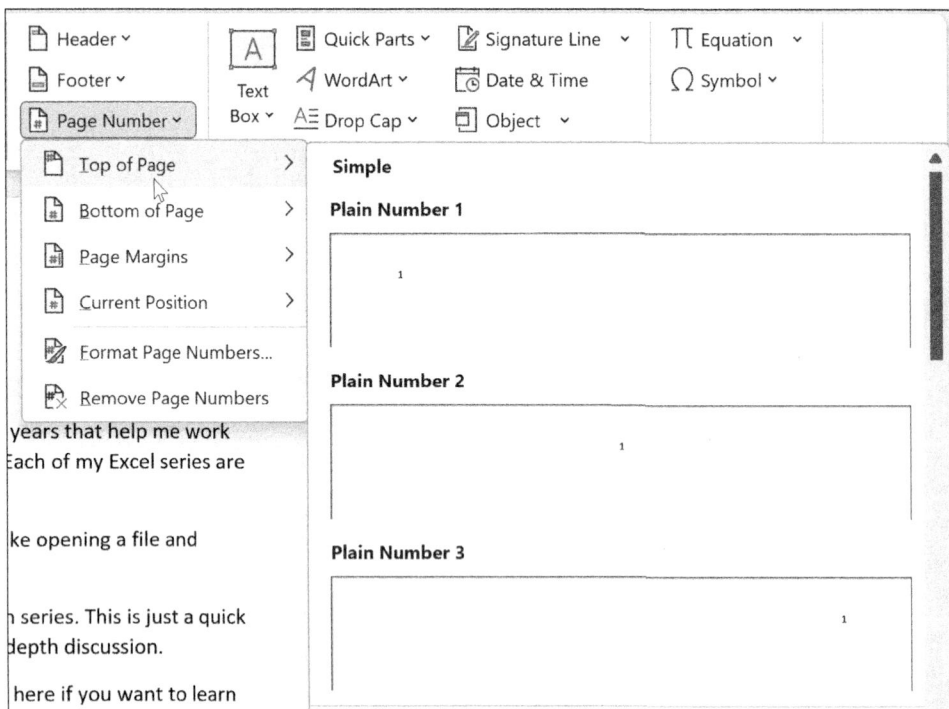

These are all locations where you can place that page number. Top of page, bottom of page, etc. And each has a secondary dropdown menu that will provide a number of options to choose from as you can see above for Top of Page.

Be sure to use the scroll bars to see the full range of choices. You can't preview the choices in your actual document, but when you click on a choice it will be inserted and formatted based on your choice. You'll also see that the header, footer, etc. section is now the section of the document that you're working in:

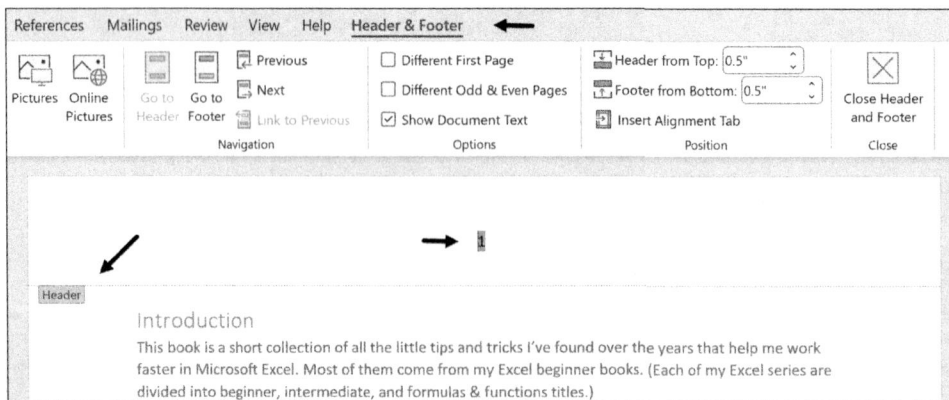

In the Header & Footer section in the far left-hand side of the Header & Footer tab is a Page Number dropdown. You can click on that and select Format Page Numbers to bring up the Page Number Format dialogue box:

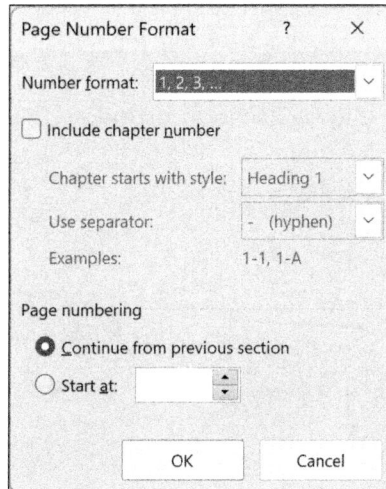

Page Number Format ? X

Number format: 1, 2, 3, ...

☐ Include chapter number

Chapter starts with style: Heading 1

Use separator: - (hyphen)

Examples: 1-1, 1-A

Page numbering

◉ Continue from previous section

◯ Start at:

OK   Cancel

This will allow you to choose a number format (1, 2, 3 vs. i, ii, iii) for your pages as well as, if needed, restart the page numbering of your document.

For example, if you have a ten-page document but the first four pages are a cover page and introductory information you may want to have page numbering start on page five but with the number 1. You can do that using this dialogue box.

For the purposes of this book, that's as deep as we're going to go with this one, but know that you can use section breaks to have different headers and footers in different sections of your document if needed. So you could have those first five pages numbered i, ii, iii and then the main body of your document numbered 1, 2, 3, etc. But that requires section breaks which are covered in the next book in this series.

To exit where you inserted your page number, double-click back onto the text of your document or use the Esc key. You can also click on the Close Header and Footer option in the Header & Footer tab.

To return to editing your page number, right-click on where the page number is and choose Edit Header or Edit Footer, whichever option appears. If you put a page number into the margins, you will likely need to right-click where the header or footer would go to get back to editing that page number.

Another option is to double-click on the page number to re-open the header or footer, but for page numbers I find that unreliable.

Page Orientation

By default documents in Word are in Portrait orientation, meaning that the longer edge of the page is on the side and the shorter edge is along the top of the page. If you ever need to change that so that the longer edge is along the top, then the way to do that is to set the document orientation to Landscape.

One way to do this is using the Orientation dropdown in the Page Setup section of the Layout tab:

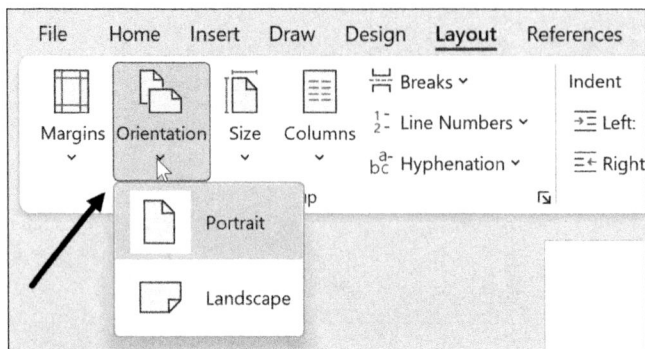

You can also do this when you go to print your document, but if I'm going to do this I usually prefer to set it that way before I start entering text and formatting.

Margins

The same goes for margins. Usually if I'm going to change those from their default I want to do so at the start not the end.

The Margins dropdown is also located in the Page Setup section of the Layout tab. Click on the dropdown arrow to see your available default choices:

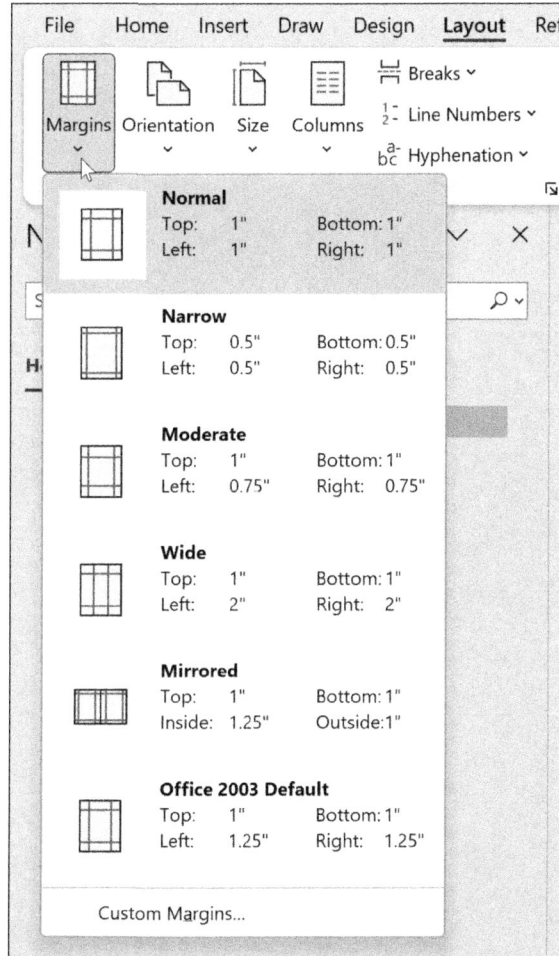

The Normal margin layout as of January 2023 is 1" on all sides, but there are options for Narrow, Moderate, Wide, Mirrored, and Office 2003 Default in that list. You can also completely customize your margins using the Custom Margins option at the bottom.

Paper Size

Another one you may want to change before you get started is the setting for the paper size you're going to use. This too is in the Page Setup section of the Layout tab under Size. Click on the dropdown arrow to see your available choices and then choose the one you want.

When you do so the page displayed in the main workspace will change to reflect your chosen paper size.

Appendix A: Basic Terminology Recap

These terms were covered in detail in *Word 365 for Beginners*. This is just meant as a refresher.

Tab

When I refer to a tab, I am referring to the menu options at the top of the screen. The tab options that are available by default are File, Home, Insert, Draw, Design, Layout, References, Mailings, Review, View, and Help, but for certain tasks additional tabs will appear.

Click

If I tell you to click on something, that means to move your cursor over to that location and then either right-click or left-click. If I don't say which to do, left-click.

Left-Click / Right-Click

A left-click is generally for selecting something and involves using the left-hand side of your mouse or bottom left-hand corner of your trackpad. A right-click is generally for opening a dropdown menu and involves using the right-hand side of your mouse or bottom right-hand corner of your trackpad.

Left-Click and Drag

Left-click and drag means to left-click and then hold that left-click as you move your mouse.

Dropdown Menu

A dropdown menu is a list of choices that you can view by right-clicking in a specific spot or clicking on an arrow next to or below one of the available choices under the tabs up top. Depending on where you are in the workspace, a dropdown menu may actually drop upward from that spot.

Expansion Arrow

In the bottom right corner of some of the sections under the tabs in the top menu you will see an arrow, which I refer to as an expansion arrow. Clicking on an expansion arrow will usually open a dialogue box or task pane and is often the way to see the largest number of options.

Dialogue Box

A dialogue box is a pop-up box that will open on top of your workspace and will usually include the largest number of choices for that particular setting or task.

Scroll Bar

Scroll bars appear when there are more options than can appear on the screen or when your document is longer than will show on the screen. They can be used to move through the remainder of the choices or document.

Task Pane

A task pane is a set of additional options that will appear to the sides or even below the main workspace. The Navigation pane is by default visible on the left-hand side of the workspace. You can close a task pane by clicking on the X in the top right corner of the pane.

Control Shortcuts

Control shortcuts are shortcuts that let you perform certain tasks in Word. I will write them as Ctrl + and then a character. That means to hold down both the Ctrl key and that character. So Ctrl + C means hold down Ctrl and C, which will let you copy your selection. Even though I will write each shortcut using a capital letter it doesn't have to be the capitalized version to work.

About the Author

M.L. Humphrey is a former stockbroker with a degree in Economics from Stanford and an MBA from Wharton who has spent close to twenty years as a regulator and consultant in the financial services industry.

You can reach M.L. at mlhumphreywriter@gmail.com or at mlhumphrey.com.

Printed in Great Britain
by Amazon

18838844R10020